The London–Bath mail coach, engraved by James Fittler and dedicated to John Palmer, Comptroller-General of the Post Office.

Stage and Mail Coaches

David Mountfield

A Shire book

Contents

Cover: *A detail from 'Changing Horses', after a painting by Cooper Henderson.*

ACKNOWLEDGEMENTS

Illustrations are acknowledged as follows: courtesy of Beagle Archive, pages 14 (top), 22 (bottom); courtesy of Anthony Colbert, pages 6, 13 (bottom), 15 (bottom), 19 (top), 27; courtesy of Consignia Heritage Services, page 25 (bottom); courtesy of Jim Corbett, page 14 (bottom); photographs by Cadbury Lamb, pages 7 (both), 8 (all), 9, 21, 31, 32; courtesy of the National Portrait Gallery, London, page 10; photograph by Sue Ross, page 28 (top); courtesy of the Science and Society Picture Library, Science Museum, London, page 18 (bottom); courtesy of the Scottish National Portrait Gallery, page 12 (top); courtesy of York Castle Museum, page 3.

British Library Cataloguing in Publication Data: Mountfield, David. Stage and mail coaches. – (Shire album; 416) 1. Stagecoaches – Great Britain – History 2. Coaching – Great Britain – History I. Title 388.3'41'0941. ISBN 0 7478 0554 7.

Published in 2003 by Shire Publications Ltd, Cromwell House, Church Street, Princes Risborough, Buckinghamshire HP27 9AA, UK. (Website: www.shirebooks.co.uk)
Copyright © 2003 by David Mountfield. First published 2003. Shire Album 416. ISBN 0 7478 0554 7.
David Mountfield is hereby identified as the author of this work in accordance with Section 77 of the Copyright, Designs and Patents Act 1988.

Printed in Great Britain by CIT Printing Services Ltd, Press Buildings, Merlins Bridge, Haverfordwest, Pembrokeshire SA61 1XF.

The coaching age

Although the word was often used more loosely, a coach was to be distinguished from other horse-drawn vehicles in having both a fixed roof and some form of suspension. Long-distance stagecoaches – vehicles that followed a regular schedule carrying fee-paying passengers – date from the Restoration (1660), but such services were extremely rare before the late eighteenth century and the business did not really take off until the end of the Napoleonic Wars. It reached its peak in the early 1830s and within a decade it was in rapid and terminal decline, having been rendered obsolete almost at a stroke by the railways.

A stagecoach in a snowy landscape remains a popular subject for Christmas cards, and the nostalgia that the old coaching days provoked set in within a generation of their disappearance. In the eighteenth century, however, attitudes were different. Most people undertook a journey by coach as a hideous necessity. Coaches were slow – little faster than the carrier's wagon that Smollett's Roderick Random overtook on foot. They were allegedly dangerous – accidents were common and highway robbers were sometimes encountered – and exceedingly uncomfortable. They were expensive

This coach in the York Castle Museum, though later converted for private use, is believed originally to have been a stagecoach, said to have run between Stockton and Darlington and to have been built about 1820.

'The Kendal Flying Waggon'. Carriers' wagons also took passengers – provided they were in no hurry. (After Thomas Rowlandson)

(from London to Edinburgh cost the equivalent of several months of a working man's wages), unreliable (schedules indicated day of arrival with the proviso 'God willing'), and somehow vulgar, being shunned by the gentry. Things began to change after 1755, and the introduction of mail-coaches in 1784 stimulated dramatic improvements. Stagecoaches soon adopted the standards of the mail, and within twenty years or so a remarkable transformation occurred: the public long-distance coach had become an object of glamour.

The sensational development of steam engines and railways – the vast scale of the enterprise and the speed of its expansion – has obscured the significance of this earlier 'transport revolution'. It may seem a comparatively minor affair now but at the time it seemed almost miraculous. Stagecoaches captured the popular imagination in a way that has been compared with the image of the Mississippi paddle-steamers.

Mail-coaches leaving the General Post Office in St Martin's-le-Grand, about 1830. (After James Pollard)

'Stagecoach Passengers at Breakfast', with coachmen hogging the fire. (After James Pollard)

People were amazed at the panache, punctuality, above all the sheer speed of the crack stagecoaches, and even more so of the mail-coaches as, clad in their sober maroon and black livery, they scattered sheep, clattered through toll-gates or dexterously exchanged village postbags, all without reducing speed. The 8.00 p.m. departure of the long-distance mails from London's General Post Office in St Martin's-le-Grand was a spectacle that attracted nightly crowds. Writers such as Hazlitt and De Quincey celebrated their celerity (a favourite coaching word), and their imperious drivers, whose haughty demeanour left no doubt of their élite status, were the popular idols of the day. They included a few genuine members of the gentry – sportsmen who volunteered to drive a fashionable public coach for personal satisfaction. Foreign visitors agreed that Great Britain possessed the finest transport system the world had ever seen.

Public coaching was more than sport or spectacle. It had significant effects on social and economic developments, achievements no less significant for being exceeded by the later railways. It was the first national transport system and, for the first time, it offered a faster means of overland travel than horseback. It was expensive (the railway cost about 75 per cent less in both time and money), but it did not seem so at the time since there was then nothing with which to compare it. Nor, in spite of the cost, was it as socially exclusive as is often supposed. People of all classes travelled by coach, if only occasionally.

Coaching speeded up the dissemination of news. The mail-coach broadcast news of Wellington's victories and the passage of the Great Reform Bill to the countryside, and the guard, who, unlike the driver, travelled the whole distance, was often the main source of news from the capital. Overall, coaching contributed to national bonding and made London less remote from the provinces.

Most businesses in the early nineteenth century were small. So, in general, was coaching, but London contained some very large enterprises. The largest proprietor, William Chaplin, ran over one hundred coaches leaving London daily. He employed

A stagecoach loading up in an old inn yard.

more than 2000 people and his enormous stables together housed nearly 2000 horses. Inns were both the headquarters and the staging posts for coaching, which thus delivered a powerful stimulus to the hotel trade.

Some of the advantages of coach travel cannot be measured precisely, notably the effect on business of the increased speed of communications. The growing efficiency of coaching under the influence of the Post Office after 1784 encouraged greater precision. Mail-coaches, which slashed the delivery time for letters, maintained strict schedules, and journeys that had once been vaguely calculated in days were now measured precisely in hours and minutes. Coaches introduced the idea of strict timekeeping, and it may well be true that people in distant villages used to set their clocks by their arrival.

The average eighteenth-century road looked something like this – the old Oxford–London road at Shotover Hill near Oxford. Hooves and wooden wheels required a different surface from that appropriate for pneumatic tyres.

Roads

One factor alone delayed the development of an efficient coaching service. The poor state of the roads not only made swift travel in wheeled vehicles impossible but also militated against potential improvements in other spheres, such as coach construction or drivers' skills.

In 1736, residents of Kensington were unable to reach Westminster because the two boroughs were divided by an impassable sea of mud. In more remote regions roads, as distinct from trackways, hardly existed. The roads had been getting worse since the Middle Ages and deteriorated faster as traffic, especially wheeled traffic, increased. In 1750 they were probably worse than at any time since before the Romans.

Turnpike trusts, empowered by Parliament to erect barriers and exact tolls on a given stretch of road in return for maintaining it, brought local improvements. They were rare until the late eighteenth century, but by the 1830s they controlled over 20,000 miles (32,000 km) of road. The remainder, about 100,000 miles (160,000 km), remained in the variable care of the parishes. Maintenance was performed under a surveyor, usually untrained and reluctant, by forced labour, a milder version of the French *corvée*, and the interests of the locals frequently did not coincide with the interests of travellers passing through their

	Miles
Edinburgh	295
Berwick	283
Newcastle	223
York	159
Manchester	91
Buxton	81

Liverpool	79
Chester	61
Holyhead	136
Oswestry	39
Salop	21
Stretton	7½

A milestone at Craven Arms in Shropshire.

7

A milestone east of Aberystwyth on what is now the A44.

region, which encouraged skimping. The great advantage of the turnpike trusts lay in transferring costs from residents to users. Although they appear to have been riddled by corruption and mismanagement, the trusts consistently spent far more per mile on road maintenance than the parishes, with beneficial results to coach travellers (though not to all road users: drovers, for example, hated stone roads, and the farmers of Sussex petitioned Parliament against them).

The turnpike trusts also provided the opportunity for testing experimental road-building techniques such as

Left: *A toll-house that formerly stood at High Wycombe on the London–Oxford road has been re-erected at the Chiltern Open Air Museum in Buckinghamshire. Toll-houses can often be recognised by their polygonal plan, which enabled the toll-keeper to watch the road in both directions.*

The table of tolls at the High Wycombe toll-house. It is easy to see why tolls provoked local riots, though these charges are higher than average.

BEACONSFIELD - STOKENCHUCH TURNPIKE TRUST
TABLE OF TOLLS
Payable at this Gate by virtue of an Act of Parliament passed in the Eighth Year of the reign of King George the Fourth.

	d
For every horse, mule, ass or other beast of draught drawing any carriage, coach, landau etc. Six Pence	6
For every horse, mule, ass or other beast of draught drawing any cart if the rollers be of a width or gauge of Six Inches at the least Six Pence	6
For every horse or other beast of draught or burden laden or unladen but not drawing Two Pence	2
For oxen, cows etc. Ten Pence the score and so in proportion for any greater or lesser number	10
For every drove of calves, sheep or lambs, hogs or pigs Five Pence the score and so in proportion for any greater or lesser number	5

By Order Thos. J. Reynolds
Clerk to the Trustees

8

The suspension bridge by Thomas Telford, completed in 1826, which carried the Holyhead Road across the Menai Strait to Anglesey.

those devised by 'Blind' John Metcalf of Knaresborough, who worked for the Harrogate–Boroughbridge turnpike in the 1760s. His principles were not much different from those of Telford later, and he showed his creativity in laying a sub-foundation of heather twigs on a road through a marshy region that had defeated earlier efforts.

The great Thomas Telford, future founding president of the Institute of Civil Engineers, was a very different figure. He is chiefly remembered for such vast projects as the Pontcysyllte aqueduct and the Caledonian Canal. The Holyhead Road, including the Menai Suspension Bridge, was a comparable undertaking. The 1801 Act of Union with Ireland demanded faster communication between Dublin and London, and the project, which was hugely expensive (determined to avoid steep gradients, Telford levelled numerous hills), would have been impossible without government funding. Telford was a builder on the Roman pattern, knowing little of theory and preferring to err on the side of caution. Basically, his road structure consisted of a foundation (the pitching) of large, interlocking, wedge-shaped stones, placed broad end downwards, each stone being only 3 inches (76 mm) wide at the top. On top and in between, smaller stones were laid ('about the size of walnuts'), which iron-shod wheels would tend to grind into a firm, waterproof surface. The topmost layer, of still smaller stones or coarse gravel, was the least important and in some circumstances could be omitted. The aim was a level surface with a slight camber for drainage and cross-drains at intervals below the foundation, leading to ditches on either side.

Telford's method was highly successful, but sheer cost ruled it out for the average turnpike trust. The answer was 'macadamising'. John Loudon McAdam developed his more economical methods in Ayrshire and established his unparalleled reputation and popular fame ('the Colossus of Roads') as surveyor of roads in the Bristol area from 1816. The main difference between his and Telford's roads was that McAdam dismissed the solid foundation as unnecessary. He was very particular about the size

John Loudon McAdam, the 'Colossus of Roads', painted about 1830 by an unknown artist.

of stone used, which had to pass through a ring. He claimed that a well-laid road of such material, 10 inches (254 mm) thick and raised above ground level, would bear any traffic. A stone foundation was unnecessary, even undesirable, since it lacked elasticity.

McAdam's contribution was not limited to construction. He was a powerful advocate of consolidating turnpike trusts to prevent the disconcerting variations between different sections of a road run by different trusts. Some consolidation did take place but only the strategically important Holyhead Road was maintained, for most of its length, by one authority.

With good roads, the improvement of vehicles, previously a pointless exercise, became worthwhile, and the result was a startling reduction of journey times, especially between London and major provincial cities. The figures speak for themselves but, if anything, they probably underrate the improvement, because in the earlier period timings were frequently optimistic whereas by 1830 schedules were strictly kept.

	c.1750	c.1830
Edinburgh	10–12 days	45^1/2 hours
Exeter	5 days	16^1/2 hours
Manchester	4 days	18^1/2 hours
Shrewsbury*	4 days	15 hours

* via the Holyhead Road

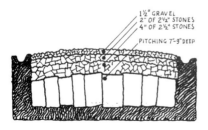 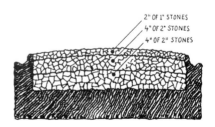

Different methods of road-building: Telford (left) and McAdam (right).

10

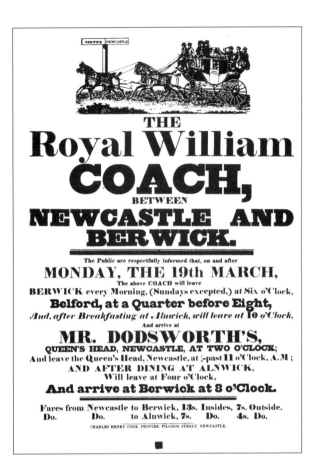

A poster advertising a coach service between Newcastle-upon-Tyne and Berwick-upon-Tweed in the 1830s.

Along with speed, the amount of traffic expanded rapidly. The number of coach services between London and major cities increased nearly tenfold between the years 1780 and 1830, and the rise in passengers was even greater, since in 1830 coaches could carry more of them. As usual, economic growth was self-generating. When demand rose to a given level, it became commercially feasible to reduce fares, or to introduce frequent stages to change the horses (woe betide the ostler who did not have the new team ready and waiting when the mail-coach drew up!), the combined result being yet greater demand and greater speed.

An early seventeenth-century coach.

Coach-building

The construction of decent roads in the late eighteenth century encouraged innovation in vehicle design. By about 1800 British coaches were widely regarded as the best in Europe, although the French might be superior in 'tasteful decoration of all sorts'. Through trade they contributed in a small way to the balance of payments: Edinburgh coach-makers exported to Russia, among other countries.

Nevertheless, much greater improvement lay in the future. Eighteenth-century coaches varied greatly but still maintained the basic structure of three units, with the

An eighteenth-century coach in an inn yard. The luggage basket and even the rounded, unguarded roof were apparently used to accommodate passengers. (After William Hogarth)

Harness for driving four-in-hand. It required considerable skill: pulling the wrong rein could cause disaster. (From John Philipson, 'Harness', 1882)

driver's box (then a flat bench) and the luggage compartment (in the form of a basket) separate from the cabin. An integrated structure did not become common until after 1800. The roof was not flat but rounded, which apparently did not prevent luggage, and even passengers, from being carried on top. Passengers also installed themselves in the capacious luggage basket at the rear. The combination of steep gradients and expanses of mud often made three pairs of horses necessary, rather than two, with a postillion riding one of the leaders. The coachman, whose seat (with the guard beside him) was comparatively low, could scarcely drive four-in-hand in any case, and the horses proceeded, at best, at a gentle trot, no doubt more often at a walk. On reaching a steep ascent, passengers were required to dismount and walk to the top.

The main technical developments of the eighteenth century were the introduction of steel springs from the 1750s (though known on private coaches in the seventeenth century) and the general lightening of construction that resulted. Early coaches were suspended from leather straps attached to vertical poles (like some ceremonial coaches today), imparting a swaying motion described with distaste by several travellers. The first steel springs took various forms, but the commonest were 'elbow' springs, attached to the body by straps and vulnerable to fracture. They were only a relative improvement. The later, hooped C-springs, again attached by straps, were

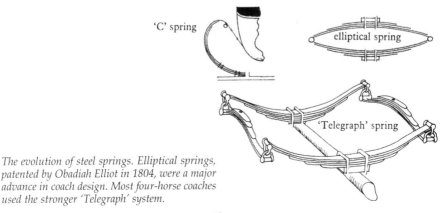

The evolution of steel springs. Elliptical springs, patented by Obadiah Elliot in 1804, were a major advance in coach design. Most four-horse coaches used the stronger 'Telegraph' system.

13

Making a C-spring.

more durable, but the biggest advance was Obadiah Elliot's elliptical springs, called 'Telegraph' springs after the stagecoach that apparently pioneered them in 1804. Elliptical springs abolished the need for a massive perch (a structure comparable with the keel of a boat), so that the body of the coach could be lowered, making overturns less frequent and further reducing lateral sway. In the same period, the driver's box and the boot were integrated with the main body, with a flat roof bearing seats for passengers as well as luggage space. The box was also raised, which facilitated driving four-in-hand – the driver controlling all four horses individually. The introduction of glass windows improved the comfort of passengers, who had previously, in wet weather, been forced to choose between travelling in darkness or getting soaked. Lamps were also introduced, providing warning to other road users rather than illumination and occasionally, especially when straw was used to keep the passengers' feet warm, the cause of fire.

A rare survival, the 'Red Rover', a coach that ran between London (the Bolt-in-Tun, Fleet Street) and Southampton (the Red Rover Inn) until 1843. It is now owned by Jim Corbett.

The Cambridge 'Telegraph' at the coach office of the White Horse, Fetter Lane, London. Booking offices in general were notoriously cramped, dark and chaotic. (From a painting by James Pollard)

Numerous other improvements continued to be made up to the end of the coaching age – and indeed beyond it – and we should remember that a simple list of developments gives a misleading picture of general progress. Technical innovations take a long time to become universal.

Brakes remained rare until the very end of the period. A coach was stopped or slowed with the 'engine', that is, the horses, and brakes were un-popular with coachmen and coach-builders. The

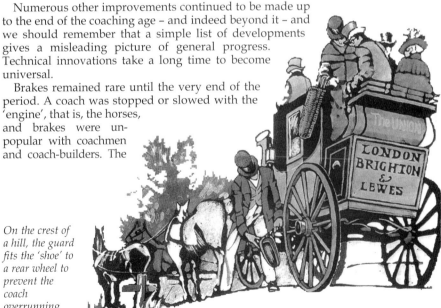

On the crest of a hill, the guard fits the 'shoe' to a rear wheel to prevent the coach overrunning the horses.

15

exception was the 'shoe' or 'drag', attached to a chain, used when the coach was stationary or descending a steep hill, when the guard would dismount at the summit to apply it. By jamming a wheel, it provided a safeguard against the coach overrunning the horses. Mail-coaches had a screw-down clamp operated by the guard by 1830, but brakes operated by the driver with a foot pedal seem to have been rare before about 1840.

The combination of better roads and faster, more comfortable coaches, and the growing business that resulted, provided the momentum for further improvement of coach services, such as the arrangement, mentioned above, for changing the horses at regular stages, which slashed the total journey time on long routes.

The major stimulus for the speed and efficiency of public coaches in the 1820s can be traced to the introduction of a system of special coaches, operated under contract to the Post Office, to carry the mail all over the kingdom. A nationwide system controlled and supervised by a government department could accomplish far more than a few private contractors could hope to do.

The scheme was the brainchild of John Palmer of Bath, who proposed exploiting the existing network of stagecoach services. Stagecoaches were much faster and more reliable than the postboys (often quite elderly) currently employed to carry the mailbags, and many people were defying the Post Office monopoly by sending urgent letters by the stage. After initial opposition, the Post Office agreed to a trial run on the London–Bath–Bristol road in 1784. Its success led eventually to a network that ran, via London, from Penzance to Thurso.

John Palmer, founder of the mail-coach system. (From a painting by Thomas Gainsborough)

Under Palmer's scheme, the operation was conducted by the same contractors who ran the stagecoaches; conveniently, they were often the local postmasters too. Profits, plus any costs that exceeded the rather tight standard rate of 3d per mile, were covered by taking parcels on an ad hoc basis, and by carrying passengers. Horses and drivers were provided by the contractors but the guards were uniformed Post Office employees. They were minutely controlled by Thomas Hasker, Superintendent of the

Time bill of the York and Manchester Mail, 4th December 1840. Strict timing was the essence of the service, but it is notable that the coach carried only two passengers: the York and North Midland Railway had opened in 1839.

Mail-coaches from 1792 to 1817, who constantly emphasised their responsibility to deliver the mail on time.

The basic system remained in place until railways took over but, to achieve the ambitious schedules laid down, it was refined and extended over the years. More frequent staging was introduced, and the time taken to change the team was reduced to a few minutes. If an accident disabled the coach, the guard would take one of the horses to carry the bags onward. By as early as 1788 delivery times for mail had been more than halved, justifying the increase in postal

The Bath Mail picks up mailbags from a village post office without stopping.

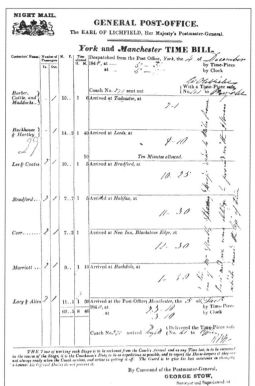

NIGHT MAIL.

GENERAL POST-OFFICE.

The EARL OF LICHFIELD, Her Majesty's Postmaster-General.

York and Manchester TIME BILL.

Contractors' Names.	Number of Passengers		M.	F.	Time allowed H. M.	Despatched from the Post Office, York, the 4 of December 1840, at — 5. - . . by Time-Piece at — 5. - . . by Clock
	In.	Out.				
Barber, Cattle, and Maddocks.	.	/	10..	1	6	Coach No. 271 sent out — With a Time-Piece safe {No. 21 to Pwysville} Arrived at *Tadcaster*, at 7·1
Backhouse & Hartley	-	/	14..2	1	40	Arrived at *Leeds*, at 9·10
Lee & Coates	2	/	10..		10	Ten Minutes allowed Arrived at *Bradford*, at 10·25
Bradford..	2	/	7..7	1	5	Arrived at *Halifax*, at 11·30
Carr........	2	/	7..3	1		Arrived at *New Inn, Blackstone Edge*, at 12·30
Marriott ...	2	/	9..	1	10	Arrived at *Rochdale*, at 1·40
Lacy & Allen	2	/	11..1	1	30	Arrived at the Post-Office, *Manchester*, the 5 of December 1840, at 3·10 by Time-Piece at 3·10 by Clock
			69..5	8	46	Coach No. 271 arrived — {Delivered the Time-Piece safe {No. 41 to ——}

THE Time of working each Stage is to be reckoned from the Coach's Arrival and as any Time lost, is to be recovered in the course of the Stage, it is the Coachman's Duty to be as expeditious as possible, and to report the Horse-keepers if they are not always ready when the Coach arrives, and active in getting it off. The Guard is to give his best assistance in changing whenever his Official Duties do not prevent it.

By Command of the Postmaster-General,

GEORGE STOW,

Surveyor and Superintendent

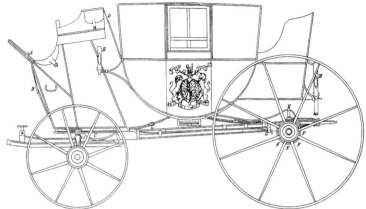

Besant's patent mail-coach of 1786. A strap from the driver's box ran under the carriage and around the rear axle, acting as an automatic brake when the box tilted forward on downward slopes.

charges. As the quantity of mail also increased, the Post Office enjoyed a substantial rise in revenue that more than matched the cost of the mail-coach system.

The first mail-coaches were no different from others, but in 1787 a standard vehicle was designed by the London coach-maker John Besant based on his patent fast, lightweight coaches. Box and body were not integrated until about 1803, which allowed the mail to carry 'outside' passengers, and it was only then that the coach began to look like the vehicle familiar from the coaching prints of James Pollard. The decision to have mail-coaches of uniform design, in formal dark red and black, gave them a distinctive identity that helped to establish their prestige. The mail was, after all, the Royal Mail, and fashionable travellers found the mails superior, more classy, as well as quicker and more reliable, than the often garishly painted stagecoaches. Later models were built and serviced for forty years by Besant's partner and

The York Mail, the oldest surviving mail-coach. Built in 1820, it was still in service under Queen Victoria – hence the monogram.

18

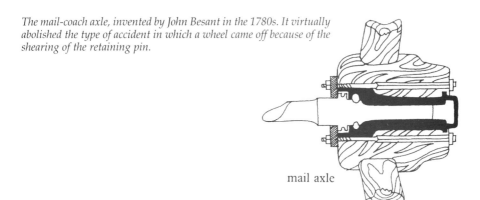

The mail-coach axle, invented by John Besant in the 1780s. It virtually abolished the type of accident in which a wheel came off because of the shearing of the retaining pin.

mail axle

successor, John Vidler, at his large coachworks on Millbank. Although the coaches bore the royal arms, they were owned by Vidler (stagecoaches too were often hired), who serviced them daily after their arrival in London, returning them in time for their 8.00 p.m. departure.

The determination of Hasker to 'keep the Duty regular' resulted in several technical improvements in coach-building. Accidents were extraordinarily frequent and many were due to technical inadequacies, broken wheels and axles being the most common problems. In the 'Mail' axle, devised by Besant, the wheel was attached to the axle by a round metal plate that fitted inside a retaining rim. It did not prevent breakages, but it greatly reduced the risk of a wheel coming off, as it often did when secured by a pin through the end of the axle. Another, less successful, innovation was a braking system that operated automatically when the coach was going downhill: the weight of the

'Insisting on the Queen's Right: "Drive through them, Watson!"'. A mail-coach driver, obeying the instructions of his guard, refuses to give way to a troop of soldiers. (After John Sturgess)

'Mail-coaches racing'. Although racing was forbidden, fierce competition on some roads encouraged it. (After G. D. Armour)

coach when tilted forward tightened a strap around the rear wheel hub. The purpose was to save time by avoiding a stop while the guard got down to lodge the 'shoe' under the wheel, but it proved less satisfactory than the older method and seems to have been little used.

Mails enjoyed certain advantages over stagecoaches. They did not have to pay duties, nor stop at toll-gates, and all other traffic was supposed to give way to them. Drivers took full advantage. Flocks of sheep had to scatter hastily, and in one incident the mail, taking an exalted view of its priority over other traffic, drove through a troop of soldiers. There were also drawbacks, since comfort was sacrificed to speed. Some people did not care to travel through the night, and there were no more leisurely dinners at roadside inns. Others found the speed excessive, complaining that there was no time to admire the scenery.

Within twenty years, Great Britain had acquired a new national institution. Inevitably, faced with such a challenge, stagecoaches also improved, exploiting the improvements introduced by the mails. The fastest long-distance stagecoaches came to compete with, in a few instances to equal and even exceed, the performance of the mails.

The coaching business

Coaching was a business with high costs, high risks and slim profit margins. No one made a fortune in it, not even the great London proprietors, whose wealth came chiefly from other interests. Coach proprietors were almost invariably innkeepers, and in the early days a coach service was often started in the provinces by a group of local businessmen eager for better communication with the capital and innkeepers keen to boost their business. It was always advisable to associate any subcontractors with the business to neutralise the conflict of interest between the requirements of the coach and the interests of the inn. To judge from the complaints of London proprietors, and of Mr Hasker at the General Post Office, the dependence on subcontractors was the bane of the business.

Although coaches, stage and mail, were generally of similar construction by the 1820s, the many individual coach-builders produced a variety of types, including an assortment of 'safety' coaches allegedly immune to overturning, as well as different styles. Edward Sherman, one of the three largest London proprietors, favoured a slightly old-fashioned design and had all his coaches painted yellow. Some proprietors also owned coachworks; otherwise they hired their coaches from the makers, at 3d per double mile ('up' to and 'down' from London). Since the cost of constructing a coach was about £140, they could run the coach, on average, for about two years before the rental exceeded construction costs. Roughly four coaches were required for a route of 100 miles, an 'up'

Richard ('Dickie') Wood, a farmer and coaching proprietor based in Doncaster, with premises also in Leeds. One of his drivers was J. F. Herring, later a well-known artist, represented in Tate Britain.

The Bear at Havant, Hampshire, on the Portsmouth Road. Former coaching inns may sometimes be recognised by a coach-sized entrance to a courtyard.

A 'Safe Coach', one of many designs intended to reduce the chances of overturning. (By Thomas Bewick)

A coach-maker's shop.

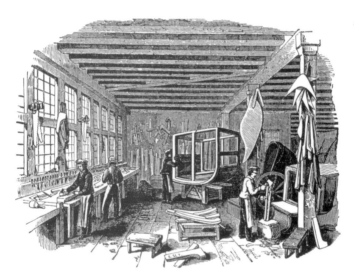

and a 'down' coach plus a spare vehicle at either end.

Inanimate vehicles were straightforward by comparison with the horses that drew them, the most costly and sometimes the most troublesome part of the business. Although Sherman horsed one coach as far as Birmingham, in general London proprietors horsed the coach for only two or three stages (say, about 30 miles or 48 km) from London. Beyond that, they depended on the country innkeepers who contracted to keep the coaches moving by supplying fresh horses and, at greater intervals, coachmen. The quality of the animals they provided varied, and in remote areas an inefficient contractor could not easily be jettisoned because there were few alternatives in the vicinity. A coachman who drove a stagecoach between Oxford and Birmingham complained constantly of the quality of horses provided at Stratford-upon-Avon. The whole team, he reckoned, was not worth £25, and the horses had probably been owned by Shakespeare. By about 1820, local landowners, attracted by the prestige of the system, often volunteered to horse the coach. They were unlikely to provide substandard animals, though there might be other less agreeable aspects to a business connection with the gentry. The cost of horsing is difficult to calculate because there were so many variables. For example, the contractors horsing the coach on a given route might all receive different rates from the proprietor, depending on the deal each one had struck.

Buying a horse was always something of a risk. Some apparently suitable animals would not go in harness, although others, too vicious to ride, might settle down as members of a team. One advantage was that coach horses did not necessarily need the qualities required for other purposes. For instance, the wheelers (the pair nearest the coach) did not need to see, and a surprising number of coach horses, even leaders, seem to have been blind. The average purchase price was about 30 guineas, and maintenance was about £3 to £4 a month (including stable hands' wages), with wide regional variations. The ideal ratio was one horse per double mile but it was seldom, if ever, achieved. It was essential that the horses were sound, as their workload was punishing. Each horse worked three days out of four doing its two stages, which together could be more than 20 miles, and, since a coach weighed about 2 tons, it was pulling about half a ton (the wheelers did more, the leaders less) over that distance. The working life of a coach horse was three or four years at best.

The literature of coaching contains references to an animal called a 'parliamentary' horse. This was a valuable beast. Galloping the horses was banned by act of Parliament (though it frequently occurred as rival coaches sought to outpace each other). However, a coachman was within the law

'The Team Gathered': the correct way to hold reins and whip. (From Edward Corbett, 'An Old Coachman's Chatter', 1890)

23

as long as just one of his team was not galloping. A 'parliamentary' horse was one that could canter at the speed that others galloped. (Some modern experts regard this achievement as improbable, and class the 'parliamentary' horse with the unicorn.)

Labour being cheap, wages were not a major item. A coachman earned a guinea a week (plus keep); a guard, half a guinea – little more than a farm labourer. However, both would undoubtedly expect to receive more in tips than in wages, and they had other, less legitimate, sources of income. Proprietors usually connived at cases of 'shouldering' – picking up and dropping off a passenger at unspecified stops without entering his name on the waybill.

The costs that coach proprietors (as others) found most irksome were the various taxes to which they were subject. Stagecoaches were taxed according to the number of passengers they were licensed to carry and paid a standard mileage duty, on average about 3d per mile, whether they ran full or empty. Similarly, the vehicle licence was calculated at a flat rate regardless of how far or how often the coach ran, and the tax on each coachman and guard remained the same no matter how long was spent on the road.

Besides the various government duties, the stagecoach also had to pay the tolls on turnpike roads, which, altogether, might add up to as much again. Returns for the London–Newcastle 'Wellington' for the year 1835 show the following costs:

Duties and tax £2568 18s 6d
Tolls £2537 7s 8d
Hire of coaches £1274 0s 0d

Income from fares is unlikely to have been more than £25,000 and was probably less, so at least one quarter of total receipts was swallowed by these three items alone.

A busy scene in the Side, Newcastle, as the mail-coach demands free passage. (After a drawing by William Heath, 1820)

An unusual accident befell the Exeter Mail crossing Salisbury Plain in 1816 when a lioness attacked the horses. It had escaped from a menagerie.

Given the heavy costs of horsing the coach, plus staff wages and incidental expenses such as advertising, fines, accidents and consequent lawsuits (one jury awarded £400 to a girl who broke her arm when the coach overturned), it seems unlikely that the 'Wellington' was making very large profits for Edward Sherman and his partners. Sometimes proprietors deliberately ran at a loss, perhaps slashing fares to drive a competitor off the road, or running an express – and thus more costly – service as a 'loss leader'.

The costs of the operation dictated what seem, from a later viewpoint, high fares. An average figure of 5d per mile is sometimes quoted, but fares varied enormously according to the region, class of coach, competition, and many other factors. On the 'Wellington', the fare from London to Newcastle was £4 10s

Highway robbery, besides being costly, was another, unquantifiable, expense, although by this date, 1827, attacks on mail-coaches, potentially the most fruitful targets for robbers, were rare.

100 GUINEAS REWARD.

PUBLIC RECORD

GENERAL POST-OFFICE,
16th July, 1827.

WHEREAS on the Night of Thursday the 12th Instant, about a Quarter-past Ten o'Clock, the Driver with the Mail between Leatherhead and Dorking, was feloniously stopped by two Men on the King's Highway, between Leatherhead and Dorking, opposite Givon's Grove, when the Men fired two Pistols at the Driver, and severely wounded him.

The Men are stated to have been dressed in dark Clothes.

WHOEVER will come forward and give such Information as may lead to the apprehension and conviction of the Offenders, shall receive a Reward of

One Hundred GUINEAS.

A Ramrod was found near the spot, and is supposed to have dropped from the Pistol of one of the Offenders.

If either of the Persons concerned in the said Felonious Attack, or any Person knowing thereof, will surrender himself, and make discovery whereby the other Offender or Offenders may be apprehended and brought to Justice, such Discovery will be entitled to the said Reward, and will also receive His Majesty's most gracious Pardon.

BY COMMAND.   **FRANCIS FREELING.**

25

PROPRIETOR	INN	MAIL-COACHES	STAGECOACHES
William Chaplin	Swan With Two Necks, Lad Lane White Horse, Fetter Lane Spread Eagle, Grace-church Street Cross Keys, Gracechurch Street Spread Eagle, Regent's Circus	Bath, Bristol, Devon-port, Dover, Holyhead, Hull, Liverpool, Man-chester, Norwich via Ipswich, Portsmouth (with Gray), Southamp-ton, Stroud (with Horne), Wells (with Fagg), Yarmouth	Stagecoaches to all parts of the country; Manchester *Defiance*, Newcastle *Highflyer*, etc.
Edward Sherman	Bull and Mouth, St Martin's-le-Grand Oxford Arms, Warwick Lane (freight)	Edinburgh, Exeter, Glasgow, Leeds, Ludlow (via Worcester)	Most parts; fast day-coaches to the north and west especially (Shrews-bury *Wonder*, Manchester *Telegraph*).
William Horne (d. 1828) and Benjamin W. Horne (William's son)	Golden Cross, Charing Cross Cross Keys, Wood Street George and Blue Boar, Holborn	Chester, Dover Foreign, Gloucester, Hastings, Stroud (with Chaplin)	Bedford *Times*, Birmingham *Tally-Ho*, Liverpool *Umpire:* fierce rivalry with Sherman.
Robert Nelson	Bell Savage, Ludgate Hill		Chiefly to the south and west; also Cambridge *Star*, Manchester *Beehive*.
Ann Nelson (Robert's mother)	Bull, Aldgate		Exeter *Defiance* and many East Anglian coaches.

Major London coach proprietors in the early 1830s.

travelling inside the coach. Outside travellers paid half that, a standard arrangement. A successful coach had to earn about £4 or £5 per double mile per month to make a profit, and a few made as much as £6 or £8, but many failed to break even.

Taxes were not the only cause of proprietors' resentment of government. Coaches were very strictly regulated. The number of passengers, the height to which luggage might be piled on the roof, the information that had to be displayed on the coach – such matters were laid down by act of Parliament, and infringements brought heavy fines. Out on the road, infringements were no doubt frequent, but they were dangerous because of the activities of informers, who received a portion of the fine when the company was convicted. Some men seem to have made a living by reporting breaches of the regulations to the authorities. A fellow in Bath reported thirty-four coaching irregularities in two weeks in 1825, which cost the Bath proprietors £500 plus costs. (The informer then wisely left town.)

All in all, coaching was a risky business, especially for small, independent proprietors. They were fast disappearing in the 1820s as, increasingly, coaches were run by partnerships that, on the major routes at least, were dominated by one of the great London proprietors.

The end of the age

The nature of coach travel meant that, by comparison with later developments, it was bound to be expensive. It could not provide the mass transit system that developing industrial Britain required and, crucially, it could not carry freight in bulk. Although the watermen were thoroughly hostile to the development of public coaching, the canal business continued to expand during the coaching age.

The stagecoach did carry certain goods, such as perishable luxuries and other small items of high value, since it was not only speedier than water transport but reached places that boats could not. The guards were well placed to profit from the speed with which they covered the country, sometimes operating a private sideline in portable articles that could be bought cheaply in, say, Yorkshire and sold at a higher price in Essex. There are stories of fencing and poaching, and it seems likely that mail guards used their firearms more often against rabbits or pheasants, even straying chickens, than against highwaymen.

The contribution of public coaching to the economy in general cannot be calculated because so many of its effects were of a kind not measurable in figures. However,

A mail-coach guard with some of his equipment, including timepiece, tools, straight horn (some preferred a bugle, top right), pistols and blunderbuss.

The number of taverns called the 'Coach and Horses' (like this one at Chiselhampton, Oxfordshire) or named after individual coaches that once called there (such as the 'Falcon' or the 'Red Rover') bears witness to the importance of coaching in the history of inns.

during roughly the first third of the nineteenth century it did make a considerable direct contribution to the exchequer, owing to the rapid expansion of coach travel. An educated guess has the number of passengers on stage and mail coaches rising by a factor of fifteen between 1795 and 1835, when the number was probably over 10 million (however, in 1870 the number of railway journeys was 336.5 million). Revenue from stagecoach duty was increasing at about 1 per cent per year in the 1790s; in the fifteen years from 1798 the average annual increase was about 3 per cent, and the rise continued at a rate of about 2 per cent per year up to the mid 1830s, peaking in 1836.

Several steam-driven road coaches made an appearance in the 1820s and 1830s and one or two services ran for a few months, but they were never a viable proposition because, apart from other objections, they were too fragile.

'Wyle Cop, Shrewsbury, A Minute to 12'. A passer-by checks his watch against the 'Wonder', which for a time competed with the London–Birmingham railway. (After John Sturgess)

A decade later, revenue had dropped by more than half and receipts from tolls showed a comparable fall, leaving the turnpike companies struggling.

In the 1830s it was becoming clear that future land transport would be driven by steam engines. In spite of some promising experiments, steam-driven coaches proved too fragile on the roads and failed to engage public confidence. Railway companies, on the other hand, proved able to attract (all too easily) the enormous investment needed to build an entirely new transport network.

The collapse of a national industry brings hardship, aggravated in this case by the speed of events. However, coaching interests, though hostile, mounted little serious opposition to the railways. Landowners and canal companies were more vociferous (waterways are said to have degenerated even faster than the roads, though canal-borne freight continued to grow for some time). Perhaps they saw the writing all too clearly on the wall, but in any case it was largely older workers and small country

29

'The End of the Manchester "Defiance"'. A once proud stagecoach serves as a hen coop, while a usurping train chugs by in the distance.

proprietors, in their emptying inns, who suffered. Edward Sherman lost £7000 in two years running the famous Shrewsbury 'Wonder' in competition with the London–Birmingham railway before he accepted the inevitable, but Sherman had a finger in many pies and became a major investor in the Great Western Railway. William Chaplin was on the board of at least one railway company. Carriers such as Pickford's were quick to transfer their business to the rails, and the bulk of the coaching workforce was absorbed by the new industry. It was easy enough for a mail-coach guard to transfer to a train, though the coachman's skill at driving four-in-hand was no use on a steam engine. Locally, some towns suffered as road traffic declined; others prospered from the arrival of a railway. The fears of farmers that collapsing demand for horses and fodder would cause a slump in agriculture and the value of land were unfounded. Laments for the disappearance of the long-distance coaches, such as Thackeray's in *Vanity Fair* (1847) – 'Alas! we shall never hear the horn sing at midnight, or see the pike-gates fly open any more...' – reflected only rueful nostalgia, not the wrath of the dispossessed.

Further reading

Most coaching literature dates from the period after long-distance public coaches had been driven off the road by the railways. It is coloured by nostalgia and is largely anecdotal. Though often instructive as well as entertaining, it tends to imbue the subject with the aura of romance encouraged equally by the prints of James Pollard and others, and it does not provide a comprehensive account of coaching operations. Few if any business records of coach proprietors have survived and other contemporary documents, such as advertisements or listings of coach services in what appear to be a number of separate services but may merely reflect the course of a single coach, are unreliable. That may help to explain why academic historians have generally avoided the subject. The most reliable studies have been those confined to a single town or region and published locally.

Austen, Brian. 'The Impact of the Mail-coach on Public Coach Services in England and Wales 1784–1840', *Journal of Transport History*, 2, 1, March 1981.
Bates, Alan. *Directory of Stagecoach Services, 1836*. David & Charles, 1969.
Copeland, John. *Roads and Their Traffic 1750–1850*. David & Charles, 1968.
Cross, Thomas. *The Autobiography of a Stagecoachman* (two volumes). 1904 edition.
Gerhold, Dorian (editor). *Road Transport in the Horse-Drawn Era*. Scolar Press, 1996.
Hanson, Harry. *The Coaching Life*. Manchester University Press, 1983.
Harper, Charles G. *Stagecoach and Mail in Days of Yore* (two volumes). 1903.
Harris, Stanley. *Old Coaching Days*. 1882.
Harris, Stanley. *The Coaching Age*. 1885.
Mountfield, David. *The Coaching Age*. Hale, 1976.
Nimrod (C. J. Apperley). *The Chace, the Road and the Turf*. 1927 edition.
Reader, W.J. *Macadam: The McAdam Family and the Turnpike Roads 1798–1861*. Heinemann, 1980.
Straus, Ralph. *Carriages and Coaches: Their History and Evolution*. 1912.
Vale, Edmund. *The Mail-Coach Men of the Late Eighteenth Century*. Cassell, 1960; David & Charles, 1967.
Wright, Geoffrey N. *Turnpike Roads*. Shire, 1992; reprinted 1997.

A notice on the wall of the Three Salmons at Usk, Monmouthshire. Crack stagecoach and mail drivers expected the ostler to wait on them.

Places to visit

Coaches or related items may be seen at the following museums but displays are sometimes changed and, before travelling, readers should confirm that relevant items will be on show and also ascertain the dates and times of opening.

Bath Postal Museum, 8 Broad Street, Bath BA1 5LJ. Telephone: 01225 460333. Website: www.bathpostalmuseum.org

Glasgow Museum of Transport, Kelvin Hall, 1 Bunhouse Road, Glasgow G3 8DP. Telephone: 0141 287 2720. Website: www.glasgow.gov.uk/cls

Red House Stables, Old Road, Darley Dale, Matlock, Derbyshire DE4 2ER. Telephone: 01629 733583.

Science Museum, Exhibition Road, South Kensington, London SW7 2DD. Telephone: 0870 870 4771 or 020 7942 4000. Website: www.sciencemuseum.org.uk

Stockwood Craft Museum and Gardens and Mossman Collection, Stockwood Park, Farley Hill, Luton, Bedfordshire LU1 4BH. Telephone: 01582 738714. Website: www.luton.gov.uk

Streetlife Museum, High Street, Hull HU1 1PS. Telephone: 01482 613902. Website: www.hullcc.gov.uk

Tyrwhitt-Drake Museum of Carriages, Archbishop's Stables, Mill Street, Maidstone, Kent ME15 1LH. Telephone: 01622 754497.

York Castle Museum, Eye of York, York YO1 9RY. Telephone: 01904 653611. Website: www.york.gov.uk

A notice formerly preserved at the Lansdowne Arms (now the Lansdowne Strand), in Calne, Wiltshire.